ANTHOLOGY ON CONVERSATION WITH CONSCIENCE...

INTERROGATION WITH SUBTLE WORDS ...!

SHIVAKUMAR U GANACHARI

Made with ❤ on the Notion Press Platform
www.notionpress.com

All Time Inspirators

My father, and father in law

Contents

Contents

Contents

Contents

Contents

Preface

Life is like experiential learning where each one of us learns the lessons of life without a structured curriculum. It teaches the significance of values, being truthful to the conscience, and the importance of good thought process in day to today life. Each one will mold the philosophy on life based on the culture that one gains through the behaviorism of family, surroundings, schools, and so… The purity of thoughts takes momentum shape through the culture of Guru, self-discovery, and being truthful to our conscience. It is universal acceptance that truth cannot hide for a long time, it is impossible to escape from God's binoculars. As the shadow follows us with the notice karma follows invisibly.

The anthology on Conversation with Conscience is an outcome of my conversation within my world. It keeps interrogating me with endless curiosity. The interrogations within forced me to express the experience and the observations that I have gained as a passive observer. The poems viz through light on the soul is speaking soul stay around Four, Letter to Ego, My rejuvenation SHE, Who Am I? Common Man's School, Predestined Appointment, and so on

In each attempt, we do it with intentions and try to get rewards or benefits. It is like a reciprocal approach if I extend my helping hand to you and the same kind of attitude that I should show during the required time … as a result, the scenario is forcing me to live against my conscience. Nowadays reciprocal has been redefined with a new narration in the contemporary world. Here hollowness, superstructure, and flattering expression have a better place than the candid deed and the words.

The grown-up ecosystem is guided to live with a conscience and practice values in letter and spirit. Don't walk into the rat race, comparison, or disassociate from appreciation, keep doing for self-contentment, and above all self-discovery takes life into a different world where only a handful could reach that destination.

I am very much critical of my surroundings trying to be very bold and never controlling my vocabulary in the expressions. The poems like Alas University, A Fair of Fashion Show, Colonialism Mind, Saga of Colonisation, Look at the West, Seed Responding, Bedarubombe, Defamed Blood, Anything Left out, and so focus on the DNA of slavery mindset the downfall of values ethics in education globalization is all about glorification without substance, and we have been defaming the blood of freedom fighters every day by living against the aspirations of the towering personalities.

Thus, our thought processes, language, and living style make us what we are. Karam will not go without its yield it is like time and space in life.

Date: 21 January 2023 Shivakumar U Ganachari Place: Bengaluru

Acknowledgements

With a deep sense of gratitude and everlasting indebtedness to my parents, Geethanjali, wife, and daughter Unnathi who is the source of my inspiration in my endeavours. I also express my deep sense of gratitude to my teachers who moulded my insights and thought process

Indeed, I don't have enough words to express my deep sense of gratitude to my father, Shri Umapati Ganachari, and father-in-law, Dr. H.M. Kailasalingam without their inspirations and guidance I would not have attempted writing an anthology. They are the ones who moulded my critical bent of mind and developed a thrust for research both in the English language and Education.

I, also take this opportunity to express my gratitude to Shri Soundarya P Manjappa Chairman Soundarya Group of Institutions, Mr. Keerthan Kumar, CEO SET, Bengaluru, and Dr. Vasu B A Principal Soundarya institute of Management and Science, Bengaluru for their constant support and encouragement in my academic progress

I, express my deep sense of gratitude to my friends Dr. Mallesh, Ramesh and Rajesh Kumar, Dr. Veerendra, Prof Jagdeep, Prof Hemaraju within my confined vocabulary because their relentless support and immeasurable insights have been the guiding force of writings!

I am always indebted to my friend Mallikarjun for making an excellent cover page of the book. He is known for creativity and commitment in every assignment

SHIVAKUMAR U GANACHARI

Prologue

Where is Learning?

Learning lost in classroom

Innate ability lost in mug up

Integrity lost in projection

Knowledge lost in superficial expressions

Cognitive ability lost in ICT enabled

classrooms...!

Intelligibility lost in education…

The 22nd century is the era of searching for

pioneers and value system...!!

SHIVAGEETHA

1. Guru

Never believed in dogmatism
Appreciated distinctiveness
Kept alive learning curiosity
Openness in learning and inventions
You are an intellectual giant
Blessed ALL without discrimination
You are Galaxy among Galaxy
tribute to My Guru
with my confined Vocabulary
SHIVAGEETHA

2. Visually Impaired!!

Idealistic and ignorant
Leadership lacks, the pragmatic
Abruptly inspires; for vow factors!!!
The Visually impaired thought process
Supersedes, true attainments!
Acknowledges superficial
Ends with frustrations
Is this folly or a suicide?
Realistic approach;
Persona non grata!
Interrogates, the followers in social networks
Less have the pink slip
More have red-carpet
Is this folly or a suicide?
SHIVAGEETHA

3. Karma Yogis

Environment predestined
Seed determines character
Aptly says, charity begins at Home...
Inspired by parents, stood by words
Never succumbed, by the unscrupulous
Lived by actions; awards followed
politely rejected!
Blessed am I to have Karma Yogis
Immaculate, deed and action
Inspired, countless and created
Selfless Gurus; without dogmatism!
Daunting to erase the footsteps
name sculptured on loftiest rock
Born Gurus, and karma Yogis
SHIVAGEETHA

4. Keeps Asking…!!!

Vocabulary keeps asking,
are you living with conscience?
endless debate, with intelligibility, and articulation
often sensibility; scolds' deportment
Promised to heart and mind
Never live in the midst of superficial
Upholds, democratic spirit and potentialities
Lacklustre with herd...
Often; profundity ironically,
Says, rhythming with fools!
succumbed eruditeness ...!
How long holds originality?
Keeps asking...!!!
Keeps asking...!!!
SHIVAGEETHA

5. Virtue in Virtual

Illustration sets the path
Influences and inspires
Seed visualizes character
First step the last step
Army culture reflects in virtual
Artificial disconnected ALL…
Claims advancement
Virtue in Virtual
Values covered in virtual
Appeared with photogenic
Illustrious illustrated in deed
Gift of the gap in diction
Artificial disconnected ALL
Virtue in Virtual
SHIVAGEETHA

6. A Word…!

A word for psychological impressions…
Used since the inception of civilization
For gain and exploitations!
Robust emotional intelligence
Least impact!
For Vibrant IQ creates a fuss
Vedic appearance tool for ALL…
A Word a lot to say…
Under HIM a word
Disappeared once and for all
Via media-built bridge
For the conflict of interest
Oh! God, you have not left …
Vedic appearance tool for ALL…!
SHIVAGEETA

7. Post Modernism!

Group of suites dressed leading;
Each other to showcase
their magnanimity
One said, I have been highlighting
Global issues in virtual mode…
Claims deserve the highest award!
The Second said, I have a large number of followers
in social networking and influenced the masses!!
Third said, I have been marketing a genuine
works of sensible in global markets…!
Fourth said, I have been leading herd and ask
them to search achievements in darkness…!!!
Capitalists capitalized penury
Gift of the gap, explored by words
Concreteness tool for networks
Alas! Being human persecuted by
a father language…!!!

SHIVAGEETHA

8. Where to Look Back…?

Name after like mushrooms,
Uses for conflict of interests!
Quotes and unquote on opportunistic
NAME after, dying spiritually…!!
Running shows on passing the bucks
Sycophants like; torch bears!
Blind guiding to deaf…
Darkness appreciates the light…!!!
Towering leaders
Led life, without definition
their living style defined
Footsteps made noise
We, quotes refer in words!
Instruct to follow, alas…!
SHIVAGEETHA

9. Empty Hand ...!!!

Use energy, tricks
Folly and unscrupulous act
to gain name, power and beyond words...
Explore, exploit through convenient
Languages, used given opportunity
for conflict of interests
becomes spiritual and philosophic
at the end of innings; is this mystery of life?
Being human, not required power or super
natural
Child Heart and care for the happiness
Nature given requirements
Acceptance leads prosperity
Begins with Zero ends with zero
Empty Hand, unwritten word...!
SHIVAGEETHA

10. Drama Show

Finds playwrights in each
Footsteps, character acts
With the script of Third-person...!
Explore, exploit and refer in
Contextualized usage
Truth uncovers diabolic perceptions
Lyricist and composer determines
HIS draft free from plagiarism...!!
Often, minor character plays like
an Epic one... twist in the tale
Curtain of make-up uncovers, covered
TIME sets Epilogue to readout
Playwrights play with Third Character
without the wish of HIM...!!!
SHIVAGEETHA

11. A Day Without YOU...

Connecting with mentor and mentee
Rejuvenate; faith in self-esteem
Departed of My stalwarts, jolted
My psychological emotions ...
takes me in deeper, secluded...
Their Absence, can't be filled
Conscience soothes, spiritual
Mentorship continues...
Taught me to walk in
The road not taken...
Keep faith in ability, and competency
Enjoy Life and freedom...
Disassociate with cynics
Mentorship continues to mentor
SHIVAGEETHA

12. Do We have Dare…?

Time, predestined, destiny
Act with synchronization
Perplexity, beyond imagination
Never, yield to the appeal
Keeps responding...
Don't find a word discrimination
in the dictionary of Time!
Attempted to interpret Life in confined vocabulary
Life, like the Epic character
Often minor plays long-lasting...
Inspirations, and draw a curtain
Intelligibility soothes through spirituality
Sensibility; accepts the Verdict of Time
Time, destiny act in tandem ...
SHIVAGEETHA

13. Promised Journey…

For, given promise forced you
to accept the discrimination…!
Given Special place…
Stayed, remain silent on exploitations
Swallowed pain, anguish, followed
Each instruction with respect
Journey of the promise made you
to Play the role of Karana…
worked relentlessly, proudly
said, self-made man
Walked into the path of the given road map
taught us honour listen to the honest toil
Spotless Journey; acknowledged you
HE bows down your head for clean image.
SHIVAGEETHA

14. Desolation from Appreciation

I, neither compete for success
nor look for recognitions
Unconditional Love; imbibed
work with passion
Disassociation with Prefixes and suffixes
Given courage to experiments
Brought equanimity from failures and success
I, neither compete for success nor for rewards ...
My Love and zeal ever-fixed mark
Keeps rejuvenating intellectually
Writes preface in each challenge
My attitude, defines NO
as New opportunity...!
Desolation brings cheerfulness ...
SHIAVGEETHA

15. Superficial Language...!!

Appeared deportment, attitude
Masked language...
Photogenic usage for mesmerizing
Outside Golden heart, inside rotten apple
Golden lines of Globalization...
A Place to dump in the line of
Progressivism, showing concerns
in mirror...connects people in virtual!
Ugly face, Beauty in the heart
illiterate on paper, eloquence
in expression, deed, and words
walk together...
unaware of hypnotic language
Humility, Love route of culture...
SHIVAGEETHA

16. A Few Questions within Mine

Rich by materials, poor by heart
Lavish in praise, intentions in heart
Submissive in appearance,
cynics in expressions...
Fault finder in each,
Ignorant own shortcomings
Survived by Sycophants
Look forward to resembling culture
Wander wonder everywhere
Superficial behaviour ...
Slogans, cut-outs of eradication
Abject poverty under ...
Visibility of Opportunists
The illusion of goodness, diabolic in reality...
SHIVAGEETHA

17. Alas! University

Impressions, center for
Knowledge generates and regenerate
Path finders in innovation
Upholders of ingenuity, without bias
The road not taken with relentless
Determined with academic integrity
Lived, without intellectual hatedredness
Explored the intellect for goodness
Alas! read in the pages!
Intellectual castigation customary
Sycophancy, offenders' addresses
On Quality education!
Politicization of academics
Mouthpiece of a representative!
SHIVAGEETHA

18. Endanger Species...!

Breed of truth, value system
Side-lined from day-to-day life
Tongue, words, and deeds
Mismatching in every route…!
Living under suspicious
Act with self-mileage
Scenario imminent; future generation
reads truthfulness as endangered species!
Breathing under doctored!
Tech-savvy knowledge
influenced tongue twisters
A few stands with words…!
Scenario imminent; future generation
reads truthfulness as endangered species!
SHIVAGEETHA

19. A Fair of Fashion Show ...!

Searched the meaning of
Fairness, profundity and integrity
got meaning only on superficial,
Flattering and hollowness...
Wandered, wandered everywhere
Fair of the fashion show and vanity fair
Blowing their trumpet... and ugly heart,
Preaching on photogenic...
Future generations refer to the Truthfulness
through references, use the credentials,
Credibility, once upon a time...!
Acceptability, and glorification mismatch
reflects state of cognitive
A fair of fashion show ...
SHIVAGEETHA

20. Stopped Looking Forward…!!

Covered discussions, after
Uncovered comments, a culture of
mediocre mind… mismatch a
Common vocabulary!
Look forward a mere hope
seldom in results…
Illusion spreads rumours
Stopped looking forward, keep acting
Visionary reaches through actions
Keeps faith in doers
Intelligibility and articulation
Never searched meaning of looking forward!!
Stopped looking forward, keep acting
Stopped looking forward, keep acting
SHIVAGEETHA

21. I am Succeeding…!

I started walking on the path
stopped lending my hear for
rumours, cynics, and negative spreadsheets
Feel ashamed to debate with wranglers
Discouraged the mind for fame and name
I am neither, competitor nor others my competitors
Prefer to stand remain student.!
I started walking on the path...
I declared myself...
I have nothing to prove...
I have nothing to teach ...
I have a culture to live with value system
I am succeeding
I am succeeding
SHIVAGEETHA

22. A Decade Journey

Life meets unknown
Diversified thinking build bondage
Faith on, firm footing on value system;
Seed, ambience visualizes character
Never disheartened My faith...
Mutual trust, reverence on each way
Made HIM to express jealousy...!
A Decade journey with acceptability...
Distinctiveness kept alive
My voracious reading striving
to explain the sacrifice, You have made
Boldness, intolerance on injustices shot in the arm
A Decade journey with ups and downs
Determinations, to defeat before defeat
defeats...
SHIVAGEETHA

23. Colonialized Mind...

Following in the routes of structured
Path, similar to remote life...
Sycophancies, bowing head down
goes unnoticed and acknowledged
glorified without inquisitiveness
habituated to follow than interrogative
Subconsciously inculcated
colonialized mind...
Pulse echoes the neo-colonialism words
blow a trumpet of have
unwritten constitution for elite
Written constitution for masses
Subconsciously inculcated colonialized mind
Route of academic slavery endless
SHIVAGEETHA

24. My Heartfelt Gratitude

Mythology says, birth defines
Karmas of previous birth...!
How fortunate am I ...
to be Blessed with affectionate
family, immeasurable in ALL
Partner with explicit and implicit
attitude, copycat daughter!
What to Say I ...?
My biological parents taught
alphabets of self -esteem
My father-in-law strengthens
Faith on credibility and intellect
Blessed am l in ALL
What to Say...?
SHIVAGEETHA

25. Without Title ...!!

Turned pages, footnotes
Since the inception of civilization
Handful brought magnanimity
Without the title ...!
Words beyond pages, fought
For titles but, disappeared
Once and for all
Sense and sensibility without title
Contentment lies in
dissolution from appreciation
genuineness, credibility and credentials
taller than the tallest
acknowledged without the titles
SHIVAGEETHA

26. Gadget Generation

Lost knowledge in information
School without scientific
Knowledge without sensibility
Creativity without freedom
Living under illusion
Misconception of modernism
Dexterity in adaptability
Intelligibility without ethics…
Superficial expressions
Hypocrisy at heart
Closeness in appearance
Disconnected in connectivity
Is this a real mask?
Is this real mask?
SHIVAGEETHA

27. Ah! My Horoscope…

Sooth Sayers say, hell and Heaven
Since the dawn, innocent exploited
Master key of Happiness and Hell
within Seed of thinking!!
Sayer defines with a terminology
Prescription of Attachment!
Herd instructions...
Don't frame questions...!
Convenient Shastras segmented
Drafted preface for inequality
Knowledge term used to Control
Outsiders through English
Insiders through Shastras
Piousness squeezes by Self-centred
SHIVAGEETHA

28. Immeasurable Footprints

Words, profundity humane act
Comes unstoppable...
Meditation, takes introvert
Keeps, rewinding intellectual
discussions and lingers in ear
Your eruditeness and voracious reading
Eternal inspirations
Truly, educated the educators
My deeper insights feel
Loneliness ....
Your humility, reverence
My eyesight
Eternal inspirations
Truly, educated the educators
SHIVAGEETHA

29. Globe…!!!

Nature the greatest teacher
Teaches life's lessons
Proportion wise teaching plan
Predestined plan of action
Guides, to have faith in innate ability
Unremitting efforts alone...
Stands with firmness
Walk judiciously; words echo!!
Peeing words on each step
Attempt to mess up the direction
Completeness remains deaf and dump
Faith and Love on untrodden path
Visionary appears in Galaxies!
Walk judiciously; words echo!!
SHIVAGEETHA

30. Not Being in Memoirs...

History written in absence of
Truth but failed to stop sun rays
On the truth and actuality
Unfortunate on not witnessed
ShivaSharanas, Aurobindo,
Raman marashi, Gandhiji, Baba Amte
Albert Camus, Karanth, Tejaswi, Jean Paul
Sartre;
Names, above the highest awards...
Words and writing complemented
without grammatical errors!
Their Life open books…
In Loneliness repeatedly
For missing memoir...
Footprints greater than the greatest...
SHIVAGEETHA

31. The Lighthouse

Inspiration, inspire like ignited minds
Keeps walking in untrodden path
Without rhetoric achieves the loved
Your indomitable spirit transformed
Life without influence...!
Your saintly life guides for greatness
Sensitiveness alone understands!
Light of lighthouse never ends...
Taught a lesson to show guts to
Reject, undeserved suffixes!
Your Lived life, facilitated to imbibe
The value system, guides granddaughter to
Inspire to walk in untrodden path...!

SHIVAGEETHA

32. Charity Began…

Your footstep expressed a dictionary
Don't remember ill words about others
Grown up with Upanishad lines
Truth Beauty and goodness…
Taught ambitious minds
Opens, the floodgates of unethical practice
Keep away from the mindset...
Charity begins at Home
Lingers in the ear
Honour listens to the honest toil
Learned to be grateful to All
Each meeting guides new
Lessons of Life ...
The spotless journey inspired...
SHIVAGEETHA

33. Talk to Yourself ...!!

'Nothing can be taught'
The rhythm of Practice and preaching
Move with tandem
Past connects to present
The beginning of the step visualizes
The last step...
Don't imitate the legacy to
Build Your identity...
Distinctiveness mocks
Competition ...
revert back to cynics' words
True mortification to innate
Discourage followers all the time
Keep talking to yourself...!
SHIVAGEETHA

34. The Price of Fear

Guru builds the logical ability
Through, fearless attitude
Understand core values and knowledge
Imbibe to move relentlessly
HE begins preface with Sublime
Live without overlapping of a word
HE harnesses the mind to grow without fear
Upholds values of Guru ...
Minimum learning and maximum
Instructions, follow without inquisitiveness
Fear, influence and disciple
Teaching plan of a modern classroom
Parochialism expressions...
The price of fear and the weapon of teacher...!!
SHIVAGEETHA

35. Prayer for My Dhore

Keep faith in You
Keep chasing your aspirations
Gain inspiration from the legacy
Never, try to walk in the footprints
Learn to travel in less travelled road
Substantiate Your eruditeness
Don't accept without WHY
Preparedness, and politeness All in Life
Be explicit in expressions;
Don't inculcate intellectual
Castigate for self-goal…!
Appreciate all, accept none
Freedom comes from a fearless attitude
Preparedness, and politeness All in Life
SHIVAGEETHA

36. Until I Survive...

Spending time with You like reading
Encyclopaedias taught the
Sharpness of observation skills
those days gone forever from
My Life, April and May the cruellest month
Wrote on rock ... continues to hunt
Until I survive...
Tonight, I write the Saddest lines
My breathing chants Your names
I am dumb emotionally and verbally
My intellect failed to convince
Your physical absence...
Tonight, I write the Saddest lines
Tonight, I write the Saddest lines
SHIVAGEETHA

37. God's Binocular

Interpretation, reinterpretation
through language skills,
Since the dawn of civilization
Perception defines, Good and Bad Times
Each Footsteps capture in the Binocular
A law without a scot-free, deed declares
Term of Good and bad times
Verdict of God without plagiarism...!
Sooth Sayers show the routes of
Anticipatory bail on the act and deeds
HIS Verdict ultimatum
In the remarks, our shadow takes a pause
Deed declares Term of Good and bad times
Who escapes from God's Binocular?
SHIVAGEETHA

38. Animated World...!

Education showing a destination
Through the image of mirror...!
Encourage for acceleration without
Individualism, the benchmark by comparison
Runs the learning process like;
Traveling on train track...!
Glorified copycat, subvert pioneers!
Living in animated world ...
Slave of own creations...
Gave a title Artificial Intelligence!!
Judged by past; illusion in visionary
Animation guiding to search
dark colour in dark ...
Living in animated world...!
SHIVAGEETHA

39. Unless Ends…!

Time apt, to take stand
Against foes...
Three enemies relentlessly
Sabotage aspirations of grooming
Education destroyed the innate ability
Teacher succumbed the morale
Technology accelerated to chase
Destination in darkness...!
Unless determined to hold
Individualism, and life in captive minds
Quotes to become like ... discouraged
to become of Their own...!
Slaves blow the trumpet to slavery...
Resistance alone reaches of own...

SHIVAGEETHA

40. Stay Around FOUR…!

Keep hovering around FOUR
Mould the path for Loved Destination
Self-esteem, integrity, Openness, and humility...
Keeps inspiring to walk in the untrodden path
Discourages to move with Herd and Followers!
Shows reverence on Distinctiveness...
Remain blind to ambitious, unethical practice!
Learns from All, but find a destination on own...
Brought up Ambience sets FOUR ...
The facilitator's 'Persona', strengthens
FOUR rejuvenates in each endeavour
Relentless, and Unremitting preface
Openness and humility stay phlegmatic
Stay around FOUR rest follows...
SHIVAGEETHA

41. Goggles Scholar…!!!

Goggles give information
on fingers tips… tempt
to act without a brain…
Heard content, and Herd
march complement each other
Goggles Scholar drive a car
without staring, neither understand its
significance nor distinctiveness…
Academic robustness comes
through profound meditation
information era failed to notified
Pioneers; malfunctioning leadership
Impotent to measure the Value System
Beware, Goggles Scholar arriving…!!
SHIVAGEETHA

42. Final Destination...!

Inspirational journey begins with
Hue and cry mesmerizing,
Cynics in each Footsteps
If lend the ear impulsive confusion
Writes to the preface
Be deaf and dump with saturated minds
Keep talking to yourself...
To reach destination...
Focusing on cry over spilt milk
Mere attempt to find the ocean in the desert
Follow instinct strive with faith
Collective support stands like rock
Time, uncertainty, and unpredictable
Work on war footing to reach Final
Destination...!

SHIVAGEETHA

43. Throwing Stone…!

Prepares tunes to set
The rhythm to move with
Their wheel of turning
Rhetoric expressions to divert
The composition of lyrics and dialogue!!
If tune compromises with them
Uses adjectives to narrate
Throwing stone routine act
Integrity, and profundity mere
Explicit expressions to gain momentum
Psychological tools to tune
The rhythm of their choice
Throwing stone routine act
Equanimity resists, Fear receives the stone…!!
SHIVAGEETHA

44. Saga of Colonialism

Psychological tunes continued
through mesmerisation, and photogenic
Equivocal minds mediocre performance
in distinguishing hollowness, and profundity!
Training, and trainers' heir to Colonialism
Corporate dictates to education through
Skills and employability
The Saga of Colonialism continues...
Do you think saga of Colonialism ends?
Afraid to speak authoritatively...
When confused minds facilitate in education!
Judged by external appearance
The Saga of Colonialism continues
With different terms in generations to come....
SHIVAGEETHA

45. Conscience Frequently ...!

Where are we today?
Surrounded by spies,
Walls echoes words for mileage!
Under uncovered mask integrity words!
Covered mask nepotism, and nefarious act
Professional status wakes in sound sleep
Where are we today?
Conscience frequently…
Where are we today?
Ambience visualizes more on
Monitoring without mentoring!
Comparison without compassion
My soothing words won't save the Ship
From the turbulence…
Where are we today?
SHIVAGEETHA

46. Why So…?

How paradox we are?
Address innovation, invention, and innate ability sets; the benchmark on looking at others
Promote copycat, Keeps explicit on
Comparison, competition...
Blindness on originality, and vibrancy on imitation
Our shadow lines appear to be ignorant
How paradox we are?
How paradox we are?
Reluctant to show forbearance
to know ingenuity...
Judged by more understood by a few
How paradox we are?
How paradox we are?
SHIVAGEETHA

47. Letter to EGO...

Revolution in Technology
Ensured to keep footprints on Moon
but failed to reach OUR surroundings!
Letter of Three and Six spread toxic
Enriched in information and knowledge
Messed up in Life skills...
Striving hard to produce literate graduates
Injecting toxic ideas for mileage
Uncertain, untimely, and unexpected
Ever companion... Three letters word
Spreads venom in the environment
Inclination towards unknown friendships
Through social networking
EGO politely prepares coffin and nail...
SHIVAGEETHA

48. Miles ahead …

Frequent conversation with
conscience strengthened my inner
voice and mauled negativity
often says, stimulate rejuvenation
to March the destination
commentaries, behind the curtain talks
customary in every footstep…!
Miles ahead Miles ahead
Conversation keeps guiding,
Guides to walk of a choice
Flourish to define explicitly
Discourages to take part
in debate, and discussions
Walking in the path of loved
SHIVAGEETHA

49. Tissue Paper Culture ....!!

Pages of History reminds
Towering personalities used
to set the right path... projected
them to gain benefits
As Time passed, treated them
Throwaway society
Use, reuse, and misuse of punctual
objectives of unscrupulous, and nefarious
Why so? Values on faith,
Ethos, and practice sets
the path for the cemetery?
SHIVAGEETHA

50. Revival for Survival

Among teachers' nature
The greatest teacher keeps
Guiding without a prejudiced act
Sessions teach with seasoned
Perceptions, penetrating mind
Alone understands the uniqueness
of revival for the rejuvenation
Time to say revival for survival…!
Robustness builds individuality
Educates to reverence ALL!
Visionary leadership alone percolates
Malfunctioning remains at sixes and seven
Dearth of pragmatic reflects in indecisiveness!
Time to say revival for survival…!
SHIVAGEETHA

51. Preparedness on Time Passers...!!

Frequent conversation
Conscience asked; time pass
a culture, habituated or attitude
of a shallow-minded...
Conscience repeatedly said,
Intelligible use without discrimination
The Shot cut gainers habituated Time pass...!
Time passes a culture of low calibres
Brought up on the greatest
Lesson plans, keeps igniting
to walk in laborious path
honours of Time rely upon ability
Prefers to walk on bumpy rides
Preparedness on Perplexed Verdict...
SHIVAGEETHA

52. A Feeling that never Ends…

Read, Read, and Read
Without time pass to
Find out vocabulary to
Express emotions about
Mother…! conscience
Said, how idiot you are
Unravelled persona neither defines
nor can be written!
Angels striving to replace,
utterly failed all the time
A word inspiration endless
Gave foundation for humane touch
Footprints printed on unbosom
A feeling that never ends …!
SHIVAGEETHA

53. What have I given you?

Proudly said I am a self-made man
Except birth nothing taken from parents
Circumstances ignited and forced to strive
Eldest, Met out the responsibilities
Father's word like a law for you
Educated, guided by value system
Your palm remained in given posture
What have I given you?
Maker examined you with all forms
utterly failed in HIS endeavours'
Overwhelmed by our visit
Proudly spoke about your elder's position
What have I given you ...?
What have I given you...?
SHIVAGEETHA

54. A Ship without Lighthouse

I grew up with matching
Words, preaching, and practice
Visionary with a humane touch
'Their' establishment remained
Torchbearers, generations to come!
Endless night spent on magnanimity
Treated All with par excellence
A ship with Lighthouse...
Alas! mismatched words
superficial expressions, and illusory castle
Journey without concreteness!
Segmentation with a trademark!
Bodies without brain
A word within the world, A word without
the world, A ship without Lighthouse
SHIVAGEETHA

55. Posthumously…!!!

Exploration of vocabulary
usage, contributions...
Is this a sign of guilt or mourning?
Stands at the forefront of rhetoric
Hypocritical appears only this time!
Reverence, acknowledgement like
Finding water, and vegetables in desert
Death understands a true face of love!!
Looked down upon the service...
Unnoticed apprehensions
Cried like a fish, and expressed sigh like a bird
Don't behave like a miser in kindness
Death understands a true face of love!!

SHIVAGEETHA

56. Recollected in Loneliness ...!

Recollecting childhood memories
is it leisurely spending time?
sharing emotions, feeling lonely
, or apprehensions of growing old?
Recollecting childhood memories
Is it expressing gratitude to parents?
unfolding the pages of ups and downs?
Seldom heart and mind compliment each!
Recollecting childhood Memories
The occasion of expressing gratitude to oneself
Loneliness, crying fish, and sighing like a birds
passive observer, remain introverted…!
SHIVAGEETHA

57. Age of reasons!

Often pretend and intended
Complement each …
Inventions substantiate the claim
Surviving under the shadow of manipulated
Interact each other in the darkness
Suspiciousness, and apprehensions hovering around
Negativity, sinister like a breath!
Is this an Age of opportunism or an age of rhetoric?
Art of usage, psychological creations
Exploratory reference of rumors
for whims and fancies
bear in mind, death not without eating the seed of fruits
is this an age of psychological bankruptcy?
often pretend and intended complement each
SHIVAGEETHA

58. Bedarubombe

Covered mask more influential
than an uncovered mask, knows
Flattering and attractiveness in
Appearance and acting
Uncovered mask instructs for
Social distancing practiced
Since the dawn of civilization
Globalization made to live like Bedarubombe
Inwardness overlooked;
Outwardness on demand
Articulatory accredited
Profundity, intellect, Superseded
Unconditional surrender on invasion
Globalization made to live like Bedarubombe
SHIVAGEETHA

59. Defamed the Blood

Blood, Blood lived by a word
fought with tooth and nail
for the birth right ...
Relentless, and laborious attempts
pioneered the path for
Next generation to live with head held high
Swallowed humiliation, barbaric treatment
Lived for country and died for country
What they dreamt for Motherland
They wrote in blood and drafted on rock
But our draft in sand and expressed in noise
The sweat of the Greatest poured into the ocean
Rogues, rascals, and bootleggers roused
the torch bearers of their own
Defamed the Blood, we defamed the Blood
SHIVAGEETHA

60. Seed Responding ...!

Conversation between two
followers one asked why so...?
When others on an exceptional path?
Ecosystem responded,
The attitude of spy on everyone
Spoilt sanity of profession
Your reflection responding, don't interrogate
Seed Responding...
Seed of arrogance undermined
Deportment Promised 'You' to teach
Influenced mind like an unsatisfied soul
Leadership without foresight and eyesight
Builds ideas castle in air
Seed Responding...
SHIVAGEETHA

61. Anything Left out?

Gluttony mindset endless
Attitude devastated beyond
Imagination, expressions, and insufficient
vocabulary, nightmares ahead of
generations to come
Mother earth exploited by nefarious
Literates, their wretchedness hypocritical
Anything left out to loot?
Invention and discovery
Lethal weapons in dissecting
The womb of Mother earth
Unscrupulous degree holders
Dugged underground for their thrust
Seed responds, anything left out?
SHIVAGEETHA

62. Look at West!!

Undermined, and Defamed own;
Apply benchmark of West to
Explore distinctiveness
Is this ignorance, farce, and idiotic?
Relentless propaganda on
West Model for progressive, and inclusiveness
Referred references of selective endless
Reminds sayings darkness under lights!
Lived by ancient subconscious thinking
Knowledge in the hands of a few
Said, God's language, only pure heart
eligible to read and chant!
West eruditeness read, claimed profundity
Look at the West model for progress!
SHIVAGEETHA

63. Glittering Outlook!!

Subtle outlook, appearance
Is it undercover reflections or
Showcase of true face?
Habituated to judge by the cover
than the content...
Indication of misfire of torch
Squeezed the originality; gave
Overwhelming welcome to glittering Outlook
Facial photogenic, first in the queue
Blur eyesight glorifying artificial
Look with a rich glossary!
The Passive living of Wisdom
Explicitly expressed in dumb language
Glittering Outlook blowing up the trumpet!!
SHIVAGEETHA

64. Being Ignorant …!

Living in consciousness
Ignorant, flourish Life
autocratic and bleaker horse in
Listening to others pissing words!
Profundity, intellectual robustness
brings eternal frustrations
Being ignorant spontaneous
Path of pioneers!
A life fully bliss and bless
Living in meditation inside and outside
Dissolution, disconnectedness, and detachment
Respiration seldom finds time to respond!
Incapable to remember the names around
Being ignorant, spontaneous path of pioneers…!
SHIVAGEETHA

65. Equivocal Journey

Blur foresight visualizes vision
castle in the air, Influences on
Superficial knowledge...
equivocal understanding enforces to
believe, begins to walk on sand!
The dearth of basic proficiency makes
to notify stars in bright sunshine
Equivocal boasts on futuristic!
Confused minds lack vision
Seldom shows hard and fast rules
Prefer to sets the rhythm of copycat!
Keeps compelling in search water
in the desert, and instruct to count stars!!
Think tank, erudite, around prevent the journey!
SHIVAGEETHA

66. Being Deaf...!

Lived in the world of irrational
Gluttony, cynical and discussions,
in the absence of Truth...
Nefarious minds spreads rumours,
References, and quotes for the convenience
Wisdom remains deaf, foolish part of the agenda
Being Deaf made free from apprehensions
Being Deaf made life in tranquillity...
Being Deaf rejuvenates the inner world
Keeps igniting to Fairness
Walk by firm footing in the hullaballoo
Reach destination with contentment
Discourages mind to respond
Sucks the beauty of Life...
SHIVAGEETHA

67. A Guest of the Day

Mantra, tantra, and pretention
nefarious act and react to lubricate
Diabolic Strategies ever fixed mark
for rhetoric, hypocrites
Explore each planning by burning midnight oil
lamp, forgotten our title a guest of the day!
Who understands HIS predestined Verdict?
Live life as a guest of the day,
A guest of the day reciprocal with bubbles
Butterfly, sucked the beauty of Life
We use cheeky tricks to label
Shows Parkinson in understanding
The law of cemetery
Live life a guest of the day as layman
SHIVAGEETHA

68. Be a Number One!

21st century classrooms illustrate
American boy invented mysterious
why can't Indian boy...?
Illusion regularly misguided aspirants
to chase their Shadow lines!
Futurists say Fish climb Trees
Crocodile runs like an ostrich
Be a number one to sustain
Comparison counsel to build
Mansions in desert
Impulsive attitude lacks precision
The loved path takes ordinary to extraordinary
Diagnose potentiality inspires to follow
Instinct; don't lend ear for number one!!

SHIVAGEETHA

69. An Epilogue

unscrupulous conducts
The trial of innocent, and honesty
Delivers the lecture on the value system
Keeps quoting quotes of legends
is this a universal
truth or spontaneous talk?
Humiliation, and castigation
Eternal followers of dignified individuals
The journey of civilization unfolded
Autobiography of towering personality
Abundant appendix of despicable
Articulated in well-knit
World well received in the beginning
Understood the truthfulness in epilogue…!
SHIVAGEETHA

70. ICT Cemetery!

Predestined destiny who
Dares to change? Compels
to accept the act of Karma
Blessed, written words, named around
An epilogue of Departed Souls
Often My own children stay away from
Rituals of final destination
Attachment watches cemetery Rituals in ICT!
Digital world made to live in animated
Humane touch in the touched screen!
The journey starts elsewhere...
Concludes somewhere
Death in the midst of a few
Is this Modernism, Post Modernism or, A Truth?
SHIVAGEETHA

71. Is there a Tomorrow?

Refer words wish, hope
Plan, believe in the intoxication
of tomorrow often hardly appears
sad to say, in the planning of the following day
forget the beauty of the present
enhance apprehensions …
intelligible lived loved on Time
jumbled minds walk in the uncleared path
rejuvenation used to connect past, and future
future like a flying high without
looking the ground
tomorrow like
SHIVAGEETHA

72. The Empire on Skeletons

Rhetoric quote what's here
finds everywhere, what's not
cannot find anywhere!
Impossible to write figures
the proper nouns! In nation building
Empire on Great Souls
Connected each for concerns
Built the empire of being human
Mafia's nexus with different
Titles, black sheep appears
Messiah of deprived
Masked leadership without expressions
Builds empire on blood of innocents
Reappear like a Sessions...!
SHIVAGEETHA

73. Name After!

Empire like a mud wall
Poured water defines a culture
Identity fencing, wall swallow
All forms of adjectives
Survives by quotes and statistics
Stays remain in the shadow lines
What's there in the name?
Mixed of Karma...
Efficacy builds the Empire of
Individuality, and existentialism
Pioneers in living
Discourage disciples, and Followers
What's there in the name?
Rise of promptness, fall of craftiness!
SHIVAGEETHA

74. Earth Rotates…!!

The earth sends, a loud and clear message
a common destination for All
karmas revert in the epilogue
words and act echoes in the journey
Sensible lives in Introvert
Results of the present; the seed of past
As earth, life rotates at regular intervals
Fool passes words, wisdom scanned!
Nature acts on a perspective deed of
mankind doesn't have guts to appeal!
mind works like a gateway
holds right to reserve!
Seed of character reveals the culture
Intelligibility aware the truth, folly reacts…!
SHIVAGEETHA

75. Who am I?

I am rational in appearance
Irrational at heart and mind
Who am I?
I am sane at first sight
Insane in deed and action
Who am I?
I am intellectual in rhetoric
Herd in practice...
Who am I?
I am sober in words
voluptuous at inner
Who am I?
I am saintly in expressions
Power monger in DNA
Who am I?
I am messiah to deprived
Sycophant of have
Who am I?
I am Gandhiji in reference
Hitler in living
I am scrupulous in Index
Unscrupulous in letter and spirit

Who am I?

SHIVAGEETHA

76. SHE...

I work relentlessly without
pretention, and intentions
Borderless word keeps adding Prefixes
and suffixes to my proper noun...
Tradition setters assigned
Multiple roles with faith on ability
Intolerant on outcomes...!
Called with multifarious names
My label used to define character,
legacy of the fraternity...
The character of individual interpret
On their education, and culture
Called with different terms
Intellect added words to the dictionary
Maye, Shakti, Demon, Earth
Wisdom act in letter and spirits
Cynics stands with words ...!
Society referred by titles...
SHIVAGEETHA

77. Do I have a Glossary…?

Taught me a culture without
Giving a series of lecture
Her living style communicated
Better than the epic!
Often cried in the rain
Made us happy all the time
Do I have a glossary to?
Express the distinctiveness
Worked, and lived like cartwheel
Never expressed displeasure from
The verdict of her better half
Mother immeasurable word
My life full of blessed and blissed
Do I have a glossary to?
Express the distinctiveness
SHIVAGEETHA

78. Money Speaks…!

Money interrogated within;
told, I am principled in words
unethical in practice!
Unscrupulous refers money
to climb position ladder
Earnest climb with perseverance
Wisdom's money speaks for Fairness
Despicable keeps tossing on intellectual
slavery…
Legacy perpetually reminds
Insane used materialistic robustness
to succumb the clean hand
Intelligibility matures to respond
Beware money speaks…
Beware money speaks…

SHIVAGEETHA

79. Journey Reminds...!

Karma reaps the fruits in
each step, enforce to understand
The yield in chaotic, disarray,
HE guides to look back through
Biological children... chanting words
Introspect the beginning and the destination
of journey....
Journey reminds the footprints of Karma
Cynics, rumours, and constructive criticism
Eternal companion virtue keen for
virtuous insights, and blocks vice ideologies
Journey reminds the footprints of Karma
Tongue and mind disconnected to hide another
Man's sin...

SHIVAGEETHA

80. Days with Masters

Dullest among dulls reluctant in
Academics, illiterate in international language
Cynics, ludicrous remarks Swallowed
Tamed from the alphabet
Blessings showed path with the lightning rod
My perspectives Copywrite with You
Your principles structured my Studiousness
The Lights of the lamp never end...
Your meticulous observations,
gigantic eruditeness
Hammered my shortcomings
Explored Creativity, and pioneer culture
robustness, articulatory shaped under your lens
The Lights of the lamp never end...
SHIVAGEETHA

81. Footprints never End...

Educated on fairness, taught
Value of living in present,
Your Sankalpa Shakti in each endeavour
Everlasting inspiration in my learning
The day never passes without your names
Cries within my world
Believed Philosophy sooth
Footprints never end
Values, and distinctiveness
Understand after loosing
Is this a law of nature? or
enlightened mind?
Achievements yield of Your seed
The folly of my own, footprints never end
SHIVAGEETHA

82. Time to Say…

Brought up ecosystem
Keep on asking, where are you heading?
Indecisive in giving fairness to
intellectual robustness; stayed in the midst of
followers and equivocal minds!
Ambience visualizes, drew a line
Time to say...
Time to say once and for all ...
Intuition drafted on the prospect
Fickle verdict everlasting
Mansion without the down to earth
Bizarre deportment spreads
Apprehensions around
Time to say once and for all ...
SHIVAGEETHA

83. Don't Trust: My Name Overambitious

My name Overambitious,
Money constant companion
Values, humane deportment, and honesty
My greatest enemies
I am unscrupulous, and nefarious for publicity
My followers succeed overnight!
I am cynics of perseverance, and sincere
My name Overambitious...
My practice reveals my culture
Impotent to counter eruditeness
Crafty living My trademark...
I encourage to chase their own shadow lines
My success falls like a pack of cards
Don't Trust, my name Overambitious
SHIVAGEETHA

84. Status Indicators!

I wandered like a drone camera
Unable to capture the distinctiveness
Notified dress code, appearance, and photogenic
Side-lined, eruditeness, pioneers...
Only superficial communicators
urgently required to the duty of postman
Dress code turns unscrupulous
as a scrupulous and gentlemen....
belongings determine the status Indicators!
Sycophants like a hot cake selling
Artificial intelligence, behaviour and lifestyle
reflected as a key social indicator
Alas! world of superstructure without the substance
Is this an indicator of a hollow world?
Is this an indicator of colonial mind?

SHIVAGEETHA

85. Sparkling Pseudo Name ...

I am plain, trusted by innate ability
Encouraged to walk in pathless
My unscanned words rejected by the
Corporate standards...
Showed the world's panorama in Drona
Instructed to dance with the remote
My name failed
My pseudo name glorified with red carpet
Quotes requote appreciated
Pioneers superseded by the tech -savvy
Borrowed ideas gain rewards and awards
Pirated knowledge glorified with adjectives
My name disappeared!
My pseudo name at pinnacles
SHIVAGEETHA

86. My Rejuvenation

Your agile learning
robust my vibrations of learning!
Your attitude of counter and recounter
Guided for the acceleration of understanding
Your nonverbal articulations
Rejuvenates my inner strength
My gratitude for being my teacher!
My better half's contributions
Immeasurable in moulding
Your eruditeness
The distinctiveness guides in
Fearless path ...
My gratitude for being my teacher
SHIVAGEETHA

87. Common Man's School!!

My Dhore keeps asking
can you read? I took time to
Pronounce a cursive word!
Responded abruptly are you poor in reading?
took my nostalgic journey of
learnt corporates language with
ups and downs in
Common man's school!
What to say often truth appears
Exaggeration and mere a word!
often failed to meet out
Inquisitiveness; reminds
unreserved time to play
Her unique among uniqueness
My gratitude for being my teacher
My gratitude for being my teacher
SHIVAGEETHA

88. Eat before Melt

Life unwritten constitution
Curve, twist under covered
Being truthful to life
Explicitly express to the obnoxious
Walks with intuitions
Remain jovial in the midst of cynics
Wise live like a fool in the fool's kingdom!!
Keeping walking don't stop…
Looking magnanimous from mediocre seed
Like searching natural beauty in the oasis
Thoughts like a seed
Time, enforce to eat fruit in tandem
Be of own, don't Roman in Rome
Life ends abruptly, Eat before melt…
SHIVAGEETHA

89. Borrowed Knowledge...!

Illusion, toxic mind pulverizes
Vibration in Surrounding,
Impotent in explicit expressions
Perceptions articulated on others
The experiential fate of borrowed knowledge
Builds the mansions in a castle in the air!
The dearth of profundity on Own
Copycat live in equivocal...
Schooling ecosystem inspires
Learners to walk Own path
Vaccinating Individual Perspectives
in the mind of learners
Like showing the Ocean in the mirror
Borrowed knowledge lives in equivocal
SHIVAGEETHA

Chapter90

91. My Name Ladder

Sensible understands my appearance
Teaches comprehensively about Life!
Steady with equanimity takes to the pinnacle
My philosophy of success ever fixed-mark
Discouraged to rat race and comparison
Self-declaration, neither I am a competitor nor
others my competitors!
My name ladder, nothing exists to measure!
Valued each one endures and endeavours
Overambitious, unethical path
Deleted once and for all
Integrity, individuality reverenced
crooks' kicks after the benefit
Yet, commitment unshakable!
SHIVAGEETHA

92. Be a Composer!

Don't dance to the tune of someone
habituated, herd, and culture of slavery
Distinctiveness shows resistance
Inquisitiveness attitude receives a Batch
Arrogant, and egoistic!
Truthfulness to the passion
Elevates to a pioneer's path
Be a composer lyric falls on the tune!
Cynicism, criticism, satire like a Common
nouns on the divergent path!
Committed brain
not like a childish
Be a composer, lyrics writes an epilogue
Living in original philosophy gives
Contentment life
SHIVAGEETHA

93. Shield of Resistance

Human evolution reveals
Change, transformation
Encountered by mediocre minds
in secureness, incompetent
Spreads rumours, cynical about the
Urgency of Change
A Dearth of adaptability ruins
Constructivism foresight prospect
Visionary walks into bumpy rides
His grit, gusty attitude encounters
The shield of resistance
The Saga of civilization cocoon under
Colonialism
Competent dexterity for urgent change
insensitive in yielding, the shield of resistance.

SHIVAGEETHA

94. Say Thank You…!

The sensible mind finds Constructivism
Talks to himself all the time
Aloof in around the world
Equally, respects both sides of coin
Lifelike a book interacted with a character
Becomes the reference for Life!
Keeps responding to the appearance
Says, thank you for being part of Life
Expressions expressed by the Director
Don't react to the dialogue
Predestined Verdict like a rising sun!
Ripeness similes till the destination
Says thank you for being part of Life
Time conquers Time…!!
SHIVAGEETHA

95. Embodiment of Inspiration

Impeccable in deed and words
a culture, shadow lines spread
vibrations of ethos
You led the alphabet Immaculately on
Self-esteem, open palm, and fearless living
Embodiment continues to torch
Learned the art of creation
Walking on the pathless culture of living
Gained knowledge practiced
You created around knowledge society
Caring, and sharing integral
Your journey remained immortal
Inspiration never ends
Embodiment continues to torch...
SHIVAGEETHA

96. Who you are?

I am the enemy of all desires
Everybody displays a board
Don't enter without consent!
Will, self-realization alone
enjoys my friendship
Beginners feel like walking on
Razor's edge ...
Greedy asked who you are?
Overambitious, photogenic
Cynical about my stature
I am ugly in appearance
Child at heart!
Who you are?
My name renunciation!

SHIVAGEETHA

97. Unbosom Heart...

The greatest contentment
Served with love, a child at heart
Worked for inner happiness
Top notched objectives...
Awards, rewards delisted words...
Uninterrupted rejuvenation
Unbosom heart in deed and words
Inspiration a torchbearer...
living style beyond the benchmark
only Great soul lead...
furious against competitions,
measuring distinctiveness
Respected all, acknowledged the Individuality
Unbosom's heart continues to shine...
SHIVAGEETHA

98. Be an Observant ...!!

Nature unrivalled teacher
teaches through symbolic,
metaphorical language...
sensitive, renunciation mind
understand the seasons of nature
life's journey begins in an unknown world
gain momentum abruptly ...
life like a leap year keeps moving...
calmness talks in introverts say,
Time filters everything
The Truth invisible dissolution alone
sees truth in an unreal world!!
Don't resist with life, accept
detachment gives equanimity!
SHIVAGEETHA

99. Silence

Express gratitude for
opportunity and giving beyond!
live like a bleaker horse
jovial life ever companion
stay remain calm to cynics
and, time passes critics ...
law of nature for buzzing
Say thank you for sinister for being part!
love life without definition
Don't build houses to yourself
Be of your own, live like an unknown citizen
Don't make a documentary of your Stature!
Express gratitude for the blessings
silence indescribable...
SHIVAGEETHA

100. Predestined Appointment!

Life beyond imagination
Life and death like a comma!
spirituality says appointments
HIS Will each meet a lesson for LIFE
Don't build bridges ...
without the direction of HIM
noting acts, accept move on
Predestined like pathless
results of present! Seed of past
Selection of Seed lies on onus!
Predestined meet creation of Destiny
Fortunate defines candidly on punctuation
Live happily forever
Predestined appointments sets beginning and
End...!!

SHIVAGEETHA

Printed by Libri Plureos GmbH in Hamburg,
Germany